Beaumaris Castle is on the Isle of Anglesey, and stands on Conwy Bay opposite Bangor across Lafan Sands. It is 4 miles (6.4km) north-east of M̶e̶n̶a̶i̶ . . . 15 road, which is . . . R SH60 . . .

IN ME̶
JACOB̶
MAGIS̶
IN WAL̶
OPERA̶

Beaumaris Castle

1295. And for a further security, he repaired and fortified all the castles and places of strength in Wales, and built the castle of Bewmoris in the isle of Anglesey.
—David Powel, *The History of Wales*, 1584

Summary

Beaumaris Castle was begun in April 1295, the last of the great royal castles with which from 1277 onwards King Edward I of England ringed the North Wales seaboard from Flint to Aberystwyth. Like Rhuddlan, Aberystwyth and Harlech, it was designed on the concentric plan, with the main courtyard of the castle surrounded by a narrow enclosing ward and both of them in turn protected by a wide outer moat.

A king and his master mason: drawing of c.1250 by Matthew Paris.
(By courtesy of the British Library).

But the site chosen, on level marshy ground not far from the water's edge, enabled its architect Master James of St George to invest its concentric layout with a degree of symmetry not attained at any of its predecessors and to fill the encircling moat with a controlled supply of tidal water. It is this combination of symmetrical planning and water defences that gives Beaumaris its peculiar perfection.

In another respect, however, the visitor may find the castle disappointing. Lacking the fine skyline which their surmounting turrets give them, it is visually less impressive than Harlech, or Conwy, or Caernarfon; the castle has a certain squatness and fails to dominate its surroundings. This is because, although the work of building went on more or less continuously for some thirty-five years, when it finally ceased in the 1330s the great towers of the inner ward were still without their top storeys, while the turrets, which seem to have been intended to rise here in even greater profusion than at the earlier castles, were never so much as begun.

Ground Plan

[Ground plan of Beaumaris Castle with the following labels: MOAT, LLANFAES GATE, NORTH-WEST TOWER, NORTH-EAST TOWER, OUTER WARD, SITE OF MOAT, KITCHEN, OVEN, HALL AND CHAMBER (OVER), NORTH GATE HOUSE, STABLES, INNER WARD, MIDDLE TOWER, CHAPEL TOWER, SOUTH GATEHOUSE, GRANARY, SOUTH-WEST TOWER, SOUTH-EAST TOWER, GATE NEXT THE SEA, BARBICAN, GUNNERS WALK (OVER), MILL, SITE OF TOWN WALL, LINE OF MOAT REVETMENT, CASTLE DOCK, MODERN BOUNDARY, WALL, METRES, FEET, N. Numbered 1–16 around the perimeter.]

The unfinished Middle Tower of the inner ward.

View of the castle from the south-west as it may have appeared if completed
(Drawing by Terry Ball)

South-West Tower with 'Gate next the Sea' in the background.

There was great initial progress with the works in 1295 and 1296, and a contemporary estimate of the labour requirement for the latter year refers to the employment of no fewer than 200 quarrymen, 400 stonemasons and 2000 minor workmen. The same record (See Appendix I, p.46) enables us to say with some precision what parts of the castle were built first; by relating this documentary evidence, together with that provided by a survey of 1306, to the evidence of the structure itself we can trace the successive stages of the work. Attention is drawn to the visible indications of these stages in the descriptive guide (pp.20-45).

Figures preserved on the Pipe Rolls (the annual accounts of the exchequer at Westminster) and in the North Wales Chamberlains' Accounts (compiled year by year at Caernarfon) show a total cost for the building of Beaumaris Castle of about £14,500 between 1295 and 1330; over £6,000 of this was spent in the first six months, over £11,000 in the first five years. A multiple of 500 may be used to give a very rough equivalent in 1985 and on this basis the castle, unfinished as it was, must have cost something of the order of £8 million at today's values.

The castle has relatively little later history to record. It never had to withstand, for example, sieges of the kind which add so much to the story of Harlech. Like all the North Wales castles it was held for the king in the Civil War; with its surrender to the Parliament in June 1646 its active life was at an end. Some partial works of demolition are known to have been carried out thereafter, but most of the structure that was built in the years before and after 1300 has remained standing until our own time.

A constable of the castle of the name of Bulkeley first appears as early as 1440, and Bulkeleys or Williams-Bulkeleys have held the office almost without a break since the seventeenth century. Finally in 1807 the sixth Lord Bulkeley acquired the ownership of the castle ruins from the Crown for the sum of £735.

By 1925, when Sir Richard Williams-Bulkeley (1862-1942) placed the castle in the guardianship of the Commissioners of Works for preservation as an ancient monument, the moat had long been entirely filled in and the walls were so shrouded in ivy that most of their masonry was scarcely visible. Their clearance and consolidation, and the re-establishment of the moat on the west and part of the north and south sides, were undertaken during the following ten years. More recently the removal of the high southern boundary wall has immeasurably improved the view of the castle from the town.

History

Introductory

In March 1284, when the death of Llywelyn near Builth and execution of Dafydd at Shrewsbury had lately brought to an end the rule of the Welsh princes, King Edward the First laid down in the Statute of Rhuddlan the pattern of a new English-type administration based on shires and counties to embrace and supersede the historic cantreds and commotes of Gwynedd. Two of the new shires, Caernarvon and Merioneth,* had as their administrative centres the castles of Caernarfon and Harlech, both (like Conwy) newly begun in the spring and summer of 1283. The third shire, Anglesey, at first had no new castle; but from the beginnings its sheriff Roger de Pulesdon was given charge of the manor of Llanfaes, and it was to be within the boundaries of Llanfaes that the new castle of Beaumaris was eventually to begin to arise in 1295. Very probably the decision to build it was taken, and its site chosen, during a week the king spent at Llanfaes in August 1283, at the very time when Conwy, Harlech and Caernarfon were all just begun. A decision not to proceed immediately with the actual work may well have been taken at the same time; the

* It need not concern us here that a first draft of the statute had proposed to create besides Anglesey, and instead of Caernarvon and Merioneth, three shires based on the castles of Aberconwy, Criccieth and Bere.

Aerial view of the castle. Note the tennis courts which used to occupy part of the inner ward.

Top left: *Conwy Castle from the north-east.*
Centre left: *Caernarfon Castle from the south.*
Above: *Harlech Castle from the south.*

Bottom left: *Carved stone lid on the coffin of Joan, wife of Llywelyn the Great, in Beaumaris parish church (moved from the priory of Franciscan Friars, Llanfaes at the Dissolution of the house c. 1538) (Copyright: Royal Commission on Ancient and Historical Monuments in Wales).*

enormous demands made by the simultaneous construction of the three mainland castles (and in the case of Conwy and Caernarfon of the town walls also), as well as by other works like the repair of Aberystwyth, Criccieth and Castell y Bere, must have stretched the English labour and financial resources to the utmost, and the projected castle on the island could take a lower priority.

The position thus selected for the future castle of Anglesey lay close beside the existing Welsh town of Llanfaes, already long the principal trading port of the island and, since 1237, endowed with a priory of Franciscan friars, in whose church lay buried King John's daughter Joan, wife of Llywelyn the Great. Equidistant by water between the castles of Conwy and Caernarfon, Llanfaes also lay on the old overland route from Chester to Holyhead by way of Rhuddlan, Aberconwy and Llangefni, being the place to which travellers to Ireland were ferried at low tide across the channel of the Menai after riding out over the Lavan sands from Aber.

No other place in Anglesey was so well suited to become the centre of its English administration and trade, as well as filling at the same time a notable gap in the chain of coastal castles that extended from Flint to Aberystwyth.

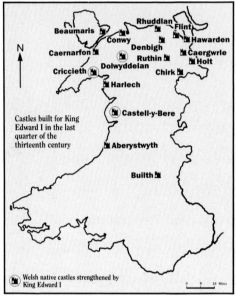

N

Rhuddlan • Flint
Beaumaris • Conwy • Hawarden
Caernarfon • Denbigh • Caergwrle
Ruthin • Holt
Criccieth • Dolwyddelan Chirk •
Harlech

Castles built for King Edward I in the last quarter of the thirteenth century

• Castell-y-Bere

• Aberystwyth

Builth •

(M) Welsh native castles strengthened by King Edward I

0   8   16 Miles

By the end of the 1280s Conwy and Harlech were finished and Caernarfon well advanced. In terms of building resources the way therefore now lay open to undertake the building of the final castle in the series planned in 1283, and the founding of the new town annexed to it. In the autumn of 1294 the Welsh, led by Madoc ap Llywelyn, rose in revolt against their compulsory enlistment for service in Gascony. The people of Arfon sacked and severely damaged Caernarfon itself; many casualties were inflicted on the English and the sheriff of Anglesey, none other than the king's favourite Roger de Pulesdon, was hanged. The revolt was quelled in a critical campaign in the winter of 1294-5, the re-assertion of English power being immediately demonstrated by the eviction of the whole Welsh population of Llanfaes and the commencement on the 'fair marsh' nearby of the king's new castle and town of Beaumaris (Norman-French 'Beau Mareys', Latin 'de Bello Marisco'). The Welsh inhabitants were moved twelve miles away to a newly established settlement, to which the name of Newborough was given, near the southernmost tip of the island.

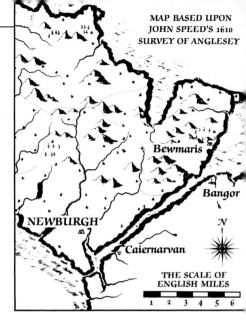

Bewmaris

Bangor

NEWBURGH

N

Caiernarvan

THE SCALE OF ENGLISH MILES

1   2   3   4   5   6

The building of the castle

1. 1295-1298 As may be seen from the table of expenditure below, the most astonishing thing about the building of Beaumaris is the speed with which the work got into its stride in the summer of 1295. Its direction was in the hands of Master James of St George, the master of the king's works in Wales, who probably like the king himself was by then a man in his middle fifties, and who already had to his credit the building of the castles of Builth and Aberystwyth, Rhuddlan and Flint, Conwy and Harlech, and, to the point at which it then stood, of Caernarfon, as well as the town walls of Conwy and Caernarfon. Such was the practical experience that Master James had at his command, ready to bring to bear with maximum effect the moment the tide of victory over revolt should enable the English to reoccupy Anglesey's south-eastern coast. The reoccupation took place on or about 10 April, from which date until 6 May the king made his headquarters at Llanfaes. There, on 17 April, Master James received 'by his own hands' an advance of 60s. for necessaries 'for the new castle', and on the following day the newly appointed clerk of works, Walter of Winchester, received the first of a series of payments which in the course of the next six months were to reach a figure of over £7,800, some £6,736 of it for the works of 'the new castle

General view of the castle from the north.

Beaumaris Castle: Table to show recorded rates of expenditure, 1295–1330

Average weekly expenditure	£	s	d
First 24 weeks, 10 Apr.—29 Sept. 1295	270	18	11
Next 52 weeks, 30 Sept. 1295—29 Sept. 1296	80	9	10
(1295–6)	(140	12	8)
Next 52 weeks, 30 Sept. 1296—29 Sept. 1297	6	7	2
Next 52 weeks, 30 Sept. 1297—29 Sept. 1298	5	3	10
(1296–8)	(75	1	11½)
Average w.e., first 3½	62	14	4
Average w.e., last 25 years	3	2	8

Total recorded expenditure	£	s	d
First 24 weeks, 10 Apr.—29 Sept. 1295	6,502	14	3
Next 52 weeks, 30 Sept. 1295—29 Sept. 1296	4,185	10	7½
Next 52 weeks, 30 Sept. 1296—29 Sept. 1297	330	12	11
Next 52 weeks, 30 Sept. 1297—29 Sept. 1298	270	2	9½
Total, first 3½ years	11,289	0	9*
1306–1330 **Total, last 25 years**	3,055	8	1
Total, 1295–1330	£14,344	8	10

*excludes £100 allocated in 1300

of Beau Mareys'. All through the summer and autumn the money poured in from Chester and Rhuddlan, from Conwy and Ireland and the Exchequer at Westminster.

Income was matched by outlay, as is shown by the following passages extracted from the fuller account of the building of the castle which is to be found in the *History of the King's Works*. In the 24 weeks from 18 April to 29 September the bills passed the £6,000 mark. In this short summer season the carriage of materials alone cost over £2,100, more than the total recorded expenditure

'bends' of iron; 105,000 assorted nails. There must already have been much to see when Edward came back in July to inspect the results of the first 2½ months' work and stayed, not at Llanfaes this time, but at Beaumaris itself; here, on two summer evenings, in a setting of temporary, thatch-roofed buildings erected 'within the castle', with the great walls and towers laid out and beginning to rise around them, the records give us a glimpse across the centuries of the king taking his ease after the day's work and listening to the playing of a harpist named Adam of Clitheroe.

Section from Building Accounts for Beaumaris Castle, 1295. Amongst others mentioned are wages for diggers and minor workmen digging trenches and excavating the moat (By courtesy of the Public Records Office).

on this item at Conwy, Harlech or Caernarfon throughout the 1280s. Here most of the building stone had to be fetched from a distance by water, both from Penmon and from beyond Benllech, and a naval force was kept in being till mid-July 'to keep the sea between Snowdon and Anglesey'. In the same period the wages of workmen digging trenches and excavating the moat and also, at the king's order, putting up a barricade round the site of the new castle, amounted to no less than £1,468 12s. 0d., indicating that their numbers throughout the summer must have averaged something like 1,800 men. Similarly of stonemasons' wages totalling £1,005 and quarries' totalling £636 point to numbers in these categories of 450 and 375 men respectively; the tonnage of stone quarried and shipped and worked and laid by them must have been immense. The quantities of materials other than stone are itemized in the surviving accounts and some details may be given here: 2,428 tons of sea-coal, for burning lime; 640 quarters of charcoal; 42 masons' axes; 3,277 boards; ropes, cords and chains; 8 loads of lead; 160 pounds of tin; 314

By great good fortune there has survived a letter sent in February 1296 by James St George and Walter of Winchester to the officials of the exchequer at Westminster, reporting in detail on what had been achieved since the previous April, and giving an estimate of how much money would

Statue of King Edward I at Lincoln Cathedral.

be needed if the pace of construction was to be maintained through the new building season that would shortly be commencing.* Already the curtain wall of the inner ward stood in places to a height of 28 feet (8.4m) and was nowhere less than 20 feet (6.1m); four of the main inner ward towers had been begun, i.e. two on either side of the north and south gatehouse passages; four gates are in position and are shut and locked at night; each gate-passage is to have three portcullises; ten smaller towers have been begun out of the sixteen which will eventually flank the curtain of the outer ward; it is implied that work is in hand on the castle dock, which will allow a 40-ton vessel to come fully laden right up to the

* The full text of the letter is given in translation on p.46.

Fifteenth-century French manuscript drawing showing the use of helicoidal (spiral) scaffolding in the building of round castle towers such as those at Beaumaris (see p. 40) (By courtesy of the British Library).

Detail of the castle dock from a painting by Alan Sorrell, showing the castle as it might have looked if finished.

gate of the castle at high tide. All this has required the efforts of 400 masons, 200 quarrymen, 30 smiths, an unspecified number of carpenters and 2,000 labourers; 30 boats, 60 waggons and 100 carts have been employed in bringing stone to the site and transporting coal for the lime kilns.

To keep a similar labour force employed through the coming year will require the expenditure of at least £250 a week (other figures show that in the first summer it had in fact been running at about £270 a week). Money is needed urgently; payments are already £500 in arrear and men are leaving the site because they have nothing to live on.

In the event, the 1295 level of expenditure was not approached again. In the second summer, from May to September 1296, it reached only some £2,132, less than one third of the previous year's figure. Money continued to run short and on the 7th of May there was not enough to pay all the workmen. There were also debts for materials, which continued to be required in enormous quantities, as for example 16,200 freestones

Iron ring for vessels to tie up to on the eastern wall of the castle dock (Illustration by John Banbury).

quarried by four contractors, and 32,583 tons of stone transported by sea to the castle. But the king's increasing commitments to Scotland inevitably diminished the resources available for Wales, and expenditure dwindled until after the end of the 1298 building season it appears to have almost ceased; we have only the record of a single assignment of £100 for the works in October 1300.

The building of the castle

2. 1306-1330 We hear no more of Beaumaris until 1306. In that year a newly appointed constable reported on the state of the far from finished castle and made recommendations for improving its security. The indications are that up to this time the outer curtain and its towers had not advanced beyond the work done in the summer of 1295; in other words only ten towers (numbered 1 to 10 on the plan at the end of the guide), with the corresponding lengths of curtain wall, had been even begun, and still stood only to a height of about 8 feet (2.4m) above the water of the moat; towers 11 to 16 with their linking lengths of curtain had yet to be started, so that on the north and north-west the castle was still left without any outer ring of defence. What was therefore urgently needed, said the report (which is in Norman-French), was (i) a good, strong barbican to cover the gate towards the dock, and at the other gate either the same thing or a good barricade *(a la porte dever Le Porth . . . une bone Barbecane e forte, e al autre ensement o bones barres)*; (ii) the portcullises (mentioned in the letter of 1296) were still needed; and (iii) it would still be necessary to complete the closing in of the castle on the north and north-west either with a wall of stone or failing that a strong palisade. Other recommendations were to repair the gates and change their locks; to scour and deepen the moat; to clean out the drains and the basements of the towers (rather suggesting that they may have been then, as now, open to the sky); and to repair and roof over the latrines (see pp.37-38), evidently then, as now, likewise exposed to the elements.

Barbican on the front of the South Gatehouse.

What, then, was done? The barbican was duly built against the front of the South Gatehouse, direct access to the gate passage of which it intentionally impedes; its round rear-arch is a Savoyard feature, suggesting completion before 1309, in which year Master James of St George died. The entrance to the North Gatehouse, at

The round rear arch of the barbican (Illustration by John Banbury).

that time still the more exposed of the two, was blocked up: in May 1306 a mason and four labourers were paid 'for obstructing the gate towards the field' *(obstruenti portam versus campum)*, and remains of the blocking walls they built against the sides of the gate passage can still be seen today. These works, the barbican in front

Remains of the blocking walls in the passage of the North Gatehouse.

of the south and the barricade in the north gate passage, would have compensated for the absence of the six portcullises, most of which could not have been installed until later, when the superstructures needed for hanging and working them had been built to the requisite height.

The urgent improvement of the unfinished defences at this time was part of a programme for bringing the castle into full commission in a period when there was fear of the Scots making common cause with the Welsh and effecting a landing on the North Wales coast. In April 1306 the constable went on a 40-day visit to London to buy armour and other supplies for the castle garrison, his purchases including a breviary for use in the chapel and 22 baldrics or belts covered with red leather. In June a mason named William de Kyrkebi was paid 3s. 9d. for shaping 180 round stones at the Penmon quarry 'for the prince's engines in the castle'; in August he received 3s. 4d. for another 160 round stones 'for the trebuchets in the castle'.

Stone balls used as ammunition for a trebuchet or stone-throwing catapult (Illustration by John Banbury).

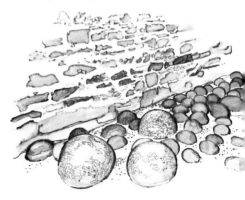

James of St George was succeeded at Beaumaris by Master Nicholas de Derneford, who had come to join Master James after previously working at St Augustine's Abbey, Bristol, the abbey of Burton in Staffordshire and Repton Priory in Derbyshire. It is perhaps to Derneford's hand that we should ascribe the unusual form of the window heads on the courtyard face of the North Gatehouse (see p. 28-31, and perhaps also the highly individual tracery of the nave windows in Beaumaris church. From 1323 his responsibilities at Beaumaris were

The North Gatehouse viewed from near the South-East Tower.

North Gatehouse window.

embraced within those of the wider office of master of the king's works in North Wales, which he continued to exercise until 1331, by which date it is to be inferred that the Beaumaris works, at least as a continuous operation, were finally halted. In general the work of the previous twenty years must have been a gradual building-up, first at one point and then at another, from where things had been left on both the inner and outer rings of walls and towers, and on the inward part of the North Gatehouse, in 1298. One major new undertaking was evidently the closing of the gap in the outer circuit from its north-east corner westwards to near the point where it had been begun on the western side in 1295, including the Llanfaes Gate and towers 13 to 16 (see plan at end of guide). There are references to completing $10\frac{1}{2}$ perches of the moat between 1312 and 1315, and in 1317 to a payment of 12 perches of moat, and these may well relate to the stretches of the moat

Unfinished front of the Llanfaes Gate.

construction of the spur wall on the east side of the dock known as the Gunners Walk. Over the castle as a whole the curtain walls, both outer and inner, were completed to the full height of their corbelled parapets. So, too, apart from those of the North Gate, were the outer towers. But for the most part the great towers of the inner ward only reached a little above the floor level of their top storeys, at which point they were left unfinished. The turrets, which would have surmounted them and given the castle as picturesque a skyline as Conwy, Harlech and Caernarfon castles, were not even begun.

The castle after 1330

Proof that, structurally speaking, the incomplete castle we see today is still very much the building at the stage at which it was left in 1330, and is not the result of decay, depredation or demolition in later periods, is provided by a report which has come down to us of a survey of Beaumaris and other castles made by William de Emeldon on behalf of the Black Prince in 1343.* Emeldon estimated that to bring Beaumaris to anywhere near completion would need the expenditure of at least £684, a very considerable sum. Nearly half of this would be needed to build the South Gatehouse, still scarcely begun towards the

alongside the new sections of wall and towers. Even then the front of the gate was left unfinished towards the field, and possibly it is this gate which is referred to in a stray document which as late as 1402 speaks of some old lead tanks being melted down to provide roofing for 'the new tower in the Outer Ward'. Probably another new undertaking of the 1310s was the

* A translation of the Beaumaris section of Emeldon's survey is given on p.47.

Detail of the north-west corner of the castle showing examples of unfinished towers.

The unfinished courtyard-facing side of the South Gatehouse viewed from the top of the North Gatehouse.

courtyard; finishing the North Gatehouse would cost £100, and the Chapel Tower £128; the other towers could simply have their roofs repaired at the existing level at a cost of £5 to £10 each. The survey says nothing of a need to erect the buildings in the courtyard whose fireplaces are still to be seen in the north and south curtains; it may well be, therefore, that these had in fact already been built before 1330, and that their disappearance belongs to a later phase of the castle's history. During the rest of the fourteenth and most of the fifteenth centuries the North Wales chamberlains' accounts periodically record minor sums spent on maintenance, but there is no evidence of work of any consequence being carried out. Nor, in the long term, was the amount of maintenance done sufficient to arrest the gradual process of continuing deterioration, especially of the leadwork and roof timbers throughout the castle. By 1534 'there was scarcely a single chamber in Beaumaris Castle where a man could lie dry', and four years later all four

North Wales castles were reported to be 'much ruynous and ferre in decay for lacke of tymely reparacons'. Writing from Beaumaris to the king's secretary Thomas Cromwell on the 9th of April 1539, Sir Richard Bulkeley reports that 'The royal castles of North Wales are unfurnished and have neither guns nor powder, nor other artillery, apart from eight or ten small pieces in Bewmares possessed by the writer. Has provided three barrels of gunpowder, some shot, forty bows, and forty sheaves of arrows, with as many coats of fence and sallets and splinters, at his own cost; this is inadequate for such a fortress. Conwey, Carn' and Hardlach castles have nothing in them to defend them for one hour. If enemies secure them "hit wold cost his majestie a hundreth thowsand of his pounds and the losse of mayny a man affor' they shuld be gotten agayn". Anglesey is but a night's sailing from Scotland. . . . beseeches a couple of gunners and some good ordnance and powder to defend the King's house in Bewmares.'

In 1609, when at least parts of Harlech and Caernarfon were still usable, Beaumaris, with Conwy, was officially classified as 'utterlie decayed'. To remedy this state of affairs, Thomas Viscount Bulkeley was later claimed by his son to have spent £3,000 in repairing the castle in aid of Charles I early in the Civil War, action paralleled at Conwy by Archbishop John Williams. From 1643 onwards, both castles occupied key positions in the transit of men and materials from Ireland to the king. For Beaumaris the eventual victory of the parliament culminated in the surrender of the castle by Colonel Richard Bulkeley to General Thomas Mytton on the 14th of June 1646, 'Beaumaris being a place that hath been of very great use to the King.' A short-lived revolt in 1648

Major-General Mytton who took the castle in 1646, from 'England's Worthies…' by John Vicars (London, 1647).

only led in Anglesey to a second surrender of Beaumaris to Mytton on the 2nd of October, and a fine of £7,000 levied on the island for its contumacy. Under the Protectorate the constableship of the castle was conferred on Major General John Jones, a near relative by marriage of Oliver Cromwell, who appointed an old Ironside officer named Captain Wray as his deputy, and annual expenditure on the garrison in the 1650s is recorded as amounting to £1,703. In 1657 we have a reference to two of its number being imprisoned 'for stealing ye leads of ye castle', which suggests a state of dilapidation, if not active partial demolition, at that time. Only a few years later, in 1665, when Lord Conway's agent was supervising the dismantling of Conwy Castle, he wrote from Conwy to his employer in Warwickshire of the dangers and difficulties encountered in taking down the lead roofs there: 'I feare I can have noe workman here that knoweth how to doe it, but I here there is one at Blewmarris that hath taken downe one or two Castels alredye, and tomorrow I doe intend to send to gett him'. Taken together, these references point to a similar dismantling in progress at Beaumaris at about the time of the Restoration in 1660, and this may therefore well have been the period which saw the removal of the medieval courtyard buildings as well as the unroofing of the hall in the North Gatehouse and what may then have remained of the tower roofs generally.

A print of Beaumaris Castle in 1742 by Samuel and Nathaniel Buck. (By courtesy of the National Library of Wales).

*Engraving of the North Gatehouse by Alfred Sumners, c.1852
(By courtesy of the National Library of Wales).*

For Beaumaris, as for the others, the eighteenth century was a time when castle ruins acquired their ivy mantles and kept the noiseless tenor of their way. Few besides the travellers to Ireland, who continued to pass by the castle until the opening of Telford's Conwy and Menai bridges in 1826, can have had occasion to observe it, for Beaumaris lacked the fame and the romantic appeal that increasingly attracted artists and writers to the more scenically beautiful castles on the mainland shore. Once, momentarily, in August 1832, the castle came into its own, when the inner ward was the setting for a 'Royal Eisteddfod', graced by the presence of Her Royal Highness the Duchess of Kent and her 13-year old daughter and future queen, the Princess Victoria.

*The Duchess of Kent about the time of her visit to Beaumaris Castle; a portrait by Henry Collen after Sir George Hayter (1798-after 1872).
(By permission of Her Gracious Majesty the Queen).*

The Borough of Beaumaris and its Defences

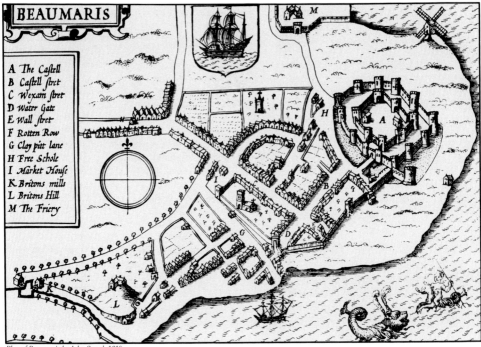

BEAUMARIS

A The Caſtell
B Caſtell ſtret
C Wexam ſtret
D Water Gate
E Wall ſtret
F Rotten Row
G Clay pitt lane
H Free Schole
I Market Houſe
K Britons mills
L Britons Hill
M The Friery

Plan of Beaumaris by John Speed, 1610.

The Borough of Beaumaris, founded by Edward I in association with the castle, whose constable was *ex officio* its mayor, was granted its charter on the 15th of September 1296. It was intended from the first to supersede the ancient and closely adjacent Welsh town of Llanfaes, whose inhabitants were removed to a new site, in Newborough, near the southern tip of Anglesey. The 132¼ burgage tenements listed in a survey of 1305 make Beaumaris the largest of the North Wales boroughs founded in and after 1278. From the beginning wine, especially from Gascony, was purchased for the other castles at Beaumaris, which soon became the economic centre, as Caernarfon was the administrative centre, of the principality. The greater part of North Wales commerce was concentrated here and distributed by coastal shipping to the other boroughs to be sold their fairs and markets. We read in 1323 of 160 gallons of Spanish honey bought for the Beaumaris garrison, and salt, corn, beans, hides, cloth, goat and calf skins are among the commodities traded. It was thus that in the fifteenth century, as Sir John Wynn of Gwydir tells

us, 'they were called the lawiers of Caern'von, the marchants of Bewmares, and the gent of Conway': if Conwy was the social and Caernarfon the administrative capital of North Wales in the later Middle Ages, the commercial capital was undoubtedly Beaumaris.

Though walled eventually, Beaumaris, unlike Conwy and Caernarfon, was not provided with its town wall contemporaneously with the building of its castle. Such provision does, however, appear to have been envisaged from the beginning. Beside the path and bridge in front of the castle entrance, and between them and the castle dock, there can be seen the 13 foot (3.9m) wide footings for a wall which at its south end inclines away to the west in the direction known to have been followed by the town wall when it afterwards came to be built. The indications are that these footings were laid at the same time as the building of the lower part of the adjacent outer curtain of the castle, i.e. in 1295, and that when it was decided, at an unknown date, that the town wall could not be built in the foreseeable future, its intended point of junction with the castle's 'Gate next the Sea' was faced up to form a low square turret projecting out from the right-hand gate tower (plate on page 21). We know that the burgesses were petitioning the king, without practical result, for their wall to be built in or about 1315.

It was not until after the town had suffered heavily in the Glyndŵr troubles at the beginning of the fifteenth century that action to remedy the lack of a town wall was finally taken. according to one generally trustworthy source the castle fell to the Welsh in 1403 and was not recovered until 1405. We have a record that in 1407 the burgesses were granted £10 towards the cost of circling the town with a bank and ditch (*in auxilium faciendi fossam circa villam*). The building of the stone wall appears to have followed within seven years, for another record, of 1414, implies that 30 burgages have been requisitioned to make way for it (*causa*

nove edificacionis novi muri circa eandem villam) so that the customary rent could no longer be obtained for them. The need for a wall to enclose and protect the town is shown by a record of 1408–9 explaining that there were 10½ burgages for which no rent could be collected, because they had been destroyed by fire not only by the Welsh rebels under Glyndŵr but also by the Scots (*eo quod combusta et destructa fuerunt tam per rebellos Wallenses quam per Scoticos*).

Only fragmentary portions of the wall remain today, marked 3 on the town-plan (below); its three gates have all vanished, as have its presumed flanking towers, It is clear that the wall was provided with battlements and latrines, and that there were passages in it. As early as 1414 ten burgages are recorded as being submerged by the sea, and in 1460 the wall itself is described as completely broken by the waves; but rebuilding is known to have been carried out between 1536 and 1540 , and the Corporation carried out repairs during the late seventeenth and early eighteenth centuries. The West Gate was still standing as late as 1785.

Plan of Beaumaris showing line of town wall (numbered references are to buildings described in Royal Commission Inventory of the Ancient and Historical Monuments of Anglesey — HMSO 1937, reprinted 1960) (Copyright: Royal Commission on Ancient and Historical Monuments in Wales).

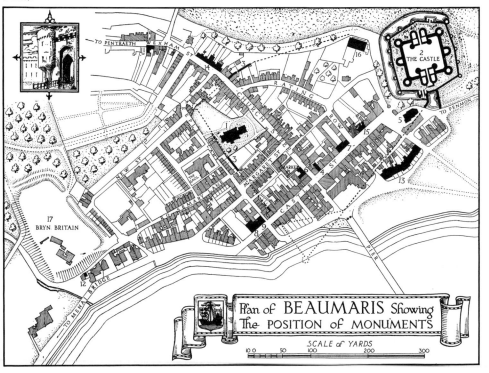

Description

Introductory

Many castles are lifted up on rocky cliffs or promontories, even though these may sometimes be only a few feet above the sea, as at Caernarfon. Beaumaris on the other hand lies literally at sea level and, lacking its own distinctive skyline, is thus denied the distant views that lend enchantment to Rhuddlan and Harlech, Conwy and Caernarfon; indeed it is only with difficulty that the castle can be seen from just across the estuary of the Menai, and Sandby and de Wint, Turner and Richard Wilson all passed it by. Today the great scale and immense strength of its buildings excite the wonder of a host of visitors, and the purpose of the description that follows is to explain as simply as possible why those buildings are planned as they are and to point out their more interesting features. First we shall make our way right into the huge inner ward, noting as we do so the various barriers — no fewer than fourteen of them — that would have had to be encountered by anyone attempting to do the same thing when the castle was in its hey-day. We shall then look at the inner ward itself, at the two great gatehouses through which access was gained to it, and at the curtains and corner towers which enclose it. Lastly we shall describe the ring of defences making up the outer ward, with a final look at these outer defences from the outside.

A castle was generally designed as a fortified residence, capable on occasion of accommodating its lord and his suite (in this case the king or the prince), and garrisoned meanwhile under the command of a constable who was the lord's deputy or lieutenant. At Beaumaris all the residential accommodation was either in, or in towers attached to, the inner ward, and the lines of defence, four in number, were ranged concentrically round it. Taking them in order from the centre they are (i) the massive curtain walls, 36 feet (10.8m) high and $15\frac{1}{2}$ feet (4.65m) thick; (ii) the outer ward, an encircling area of open ground averaging about 60 feet (18m) in width and commanded from the battlements of (i); (iii) the lower and less massive outer curtain, with its eight battlemented sides flanked by twelve battlemented turrets and pierced by two twin-towered gateways; and (iv) the water-filled moat, now only partially but originally wholly surrounding everything comprised in (i) — (iii).

The visitor approaches the castle across a modern timber bridge leading up to the 'Gate next the Sea', which contained the first three of the obstacles referred to above: a drawbridge, its

Below: *An aerial view of the castle from the north showing its overall layout.*
Right: *The 'Gate next the Sea' from the outside.*

Above: *The outer face of the 'Gate next the Sea' looking upwards. Note the two holes for the drawbridge chains near the top of the arch.*

Right: *Parallel 'murder slots' over the passage of the 'Gate next the Sea'.*

chains formerly passing through two holes still visible high up within the outer arch, two parallel 'murder slots' over the gate passage, and a heavy two-leaved door of which the drawbar hole and the stumps of the hinges can still be seen. Ahead and at right angles are the next two hazards, namely the doorway into the barbican and the barbican itself, its interior commanded by a shooting platform running round the three sides of its wall-head. The remaining nine barriers were built into the main gatehouse passage, and each may be noted in turn: outwards-opening doors, with double drawbarholes on the inside; the grooves for the first of the three portcullises; five parallel 'murder slots' overhead; 'spy holes' through which an entrant could be identified from within the towers on either side; the grooves of the second portcullis; inwards-opening doors (also with double drawbar holes visible on the inside); another row of 'murder slots' in the now missing roof of the next part of the passage, from which doors on either side led to porters' lodges and to the newel stairs to the upper parts of the gatehouse, finally, by analogy from the corresponding features of the other gatehouse opposite, came the third portcullis, with another 'murder slot' in the arch above it. When all these checks had been safely negotiated, then, and only then, was entrance to be had into the inner ward.

Right: *The second portcullis and drawbar holes of the inwards- opening doors in the passage of the South Gatehouse.*

Below: *The South Gatehouse passage looking outwards towards the barbican with the second portcullis in the foreground.*

A bird's eye view of Beaumaris Castle from the south-west

with notes on some of the principal features

1 *North Gatehouse — Had this and the matching South Gatehouse been completed, they would have been on an even grander scale than the Great Gatehouse at Harlech Castle. The lower five of what were originally intended to be ten magnificent windows face into the courtyard (pp. 28-31).*

2 *Llanfaes Gate — Built sometime between 1306 and 1330; the outer face of the gate was never completed (pp. 13 & 42-3).*

13 *Tower 1 — A point just to the north of this tower marks the building break in the construction of the outer defences noted in 4 opposite (pp. 13-14).*

12 *Outer Defence — The horizontal building break 8 feet (2.4m) above the moat water level can be seen clearly along this stretch of the outer curtain wall (pp. 11 & 42-3).*

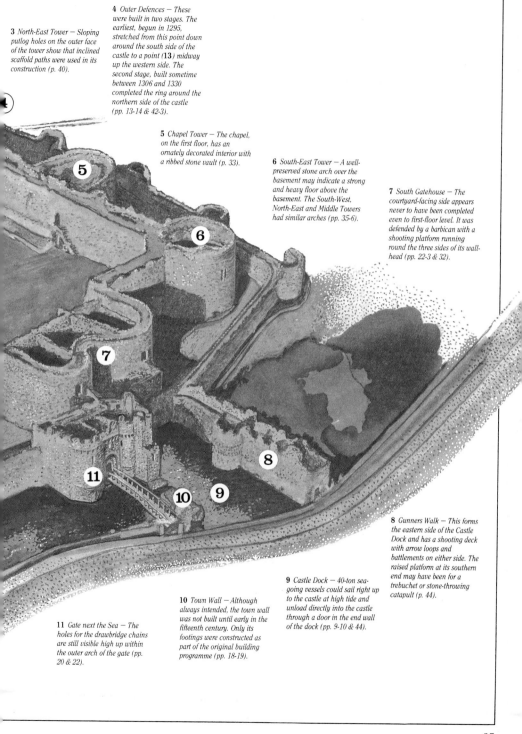

3 *North-East Tower – Sloping putlog holes on the outer face of the tower show that inclined scaffold paths were used in its construction (p. 40).*

4 *Outer Defences – These were built in two stages. The earliest, begun in 1295, stretched from this point down around the south side of the castle to a point (13) midway up the western side. The second stage, built sometime between 1306 and 1330 completed the ring around the northern side of the castle (pp. 13-14 & 42-3).*

5 *Chapel Tower – The chapel, on the first floor, has an ornately decorated interior with a ribbed stone vault (p. 33).*

6 *South-East Tower – A well-preserved stone arch over the basement may indicate a strong and heavy floor above the basement. The South-West, North-East and Middle Towers had similar arches (pp. 35-6).*

7 *South Gatehouse – The courtyard-facing side appears never to have been completed even to first-floor level. It was defended by a barbican with a shooting platform running round the three sides of its wall-head (pp. 22-3 & 32).*

8 *Gunners Walk – This forms the eastern side of the Castle Dock and has a shooting deck with arrow loops and battlements on either side. The raised platform at its southern end may have been for a trebuchet or stone-throwing catapult (p. 44).*

9 *Castle Dock – 40-ton sea-going vessels could sail right up to the castle at high tide and unload directly into the castle through a door in the end wall of the dock (pp. 9-10 & 44).*

10 *Town Wall – Although always intended, the town wall was not built until early in the fifteenth century. Only its footings were constructed as part of the original building programme (pp. 18-19).*

11 *Gate next the Sea – The holes for the drawbridge chains are still visible high up within the outer arch of the gate (pp. 20 & 22).*

Interior of inner ward

The striking thing is its size — $\frac{3}{4}$ of an acre (.3 ha). It is not difficult to picture it filled, as we are told it was filled in the winter of 1295—6, with huts to house the work force of upwards of 2,000 men engaged on the manifold tasks of construction. Its present spaciousness, however, was originally curtailed, or designed to be curtailed, by long ranges of building running the full length of its western and about half the length of its eastern sides, and by a building in the south-east corner. The lower door openings to be seen in the north-east, south-east and south-west corners and in the centre of the west side were all shaped for 'interior doors' i.e. they were to provide access to and from buildings that no longer exist against the east and west curtains; note the careful rebating of some of these openings to house flush-fitting doors. Other

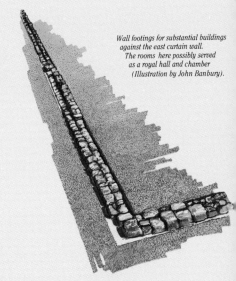

Wall footings for substantial buildings against the east curtain wall. The rooms here possibly served as a royal hall and chamber (Illustration by John Banbury).

Aerial view of the castle from the south-east.

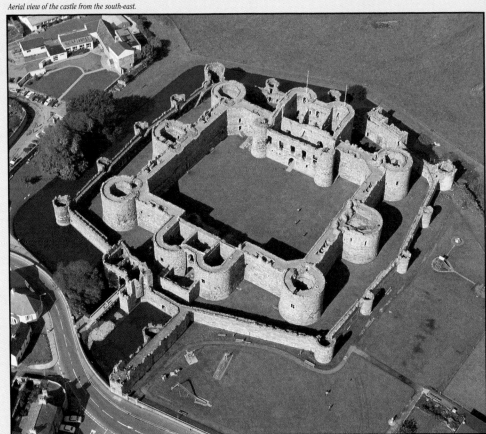

evidence on the west side is provided by the ground-floor fireplace at the north end, by two small bondings at ground level a little to the south of it, by a length of 5 feet 9 inches (1.72m) wide foundation for the inner wall which survives at the north end also, and by the offset to carry a floor which runs along the whole length of the western curtain. Very probably the northern part contained the kitchen and the southern the stables, which at Conwy were similarly placed end to end on the opposite side of the courtyard to the hall. The evidence on the east side is provided by a similar offset to be found along the northern half of the curtain only and terminating on the line of 3′6″ (1.05m) wide return wall, the bonding of which can be seen extending to full height of the curtain just south of the modern external staircase. At the level of this offset are two fine fireplaces evidently intended to serve rooms of major importance, whose windows would have been in the now vanished wall towards the courtyard; as at Conwy, their proximity to the

chapel suggests a royal hall and chamber. Beneath them was a low basement; there survives from this a partly blocked opening for light and air towards the north, originally heavily barred where it emerges towards the outer ward. The remains of an oven fill the adjacent corner against the North Gatehouse. The existence of a former south-east building is vouched for by the wall-plaster still adhering to the south curtain; clearly its end wall was the east wall of the South Gatehouse, considerably more of which must therefore have stood at one time than remains today. This fact alone gives rise to doubt as to whether, as has sometimes been suggested, the vanished courtyard buildings were indeed never built, or whether their absence may not rather reflect the activity of the 'one at blewmarris that hath taken downe one or two Castels alredye', as reported by Lord Conway's agent in 1665. We are entirely without information both as to how extensive the stone robbing may have been and as to how late it may have continued; for example, one cannot look

Part of the eastern side of the inner ward. The wooden staircase leads to the chapel.

at Beaumaris Gaol (built 1829) without some suspicion as to whether all its building stone was newly quarried for the purpose, or may not in part at least have come from the castle.

The entrance to Beaumaris gaol.

Two other features visible from within the inner ward may be pointed out. The first is a series of three inclined lines of putlog holes sloping up from ground to wall-top level over the whole length of the west curtain; these are best seen from the middle or far side of the courtyard; the holes held the bearer poles of inclined scaffold paths used instead of vertical ladders and cranes for hoisting material at the time of the original building, and the careful observer will notice them in other parts of the castle also. The second feature is the presence at wall-top level of pairs of rounded projections, near to the centre of each of the longer curtains, where they are corbelled out above the main wall face below. They apparently mark the bases of uncompleted turrets, one of which on each side would have contained the stairs to the roof of the adjacent unfinished tower. The position of the castle well, presumably somewhere within the courtyard, has yet to be discovered.

The North Gatehouse

Imposing as it is, the great North Gatehouse of Beaumaris is but a fragment of the building it was intended to be, a gatehouse of similar plan and pattern to, but of considerably larger dimensions

The inside face of the North Gatehouse at Beaumaris Castle.

The inside face of the main gatehouse at Harlech Castle.

than, the still almost completely surviving gatehouse designed by the same architect twelve years earlier at Harlech. The Harlech gatehouse has six windows, three to each floor, towards the courtyard; here there were to be ten, of which only the existing lower five were ever built, the upper five, as may still be seen (detail on p. 31) never having risen beyond the level of their window seats. Had they been completed, the height of the two corner turrets would have been approximately double the height to which they stand today, and appreciably higher than the highest surviving parts of the gatehouse, namely the two flanking towers projecting towards the

north. These alone of the great towers of the inner ward stand to something approaching their full intended height of about 60 feet (18m) and only lack their battlements and their rear walls.

At ground level, running centrally through the gatehouse from north to south, is the heavily defended entrance passage (cf. pp. 20–23); remains of the blocking structure inserted in it in 1306 (p. 12) can be seen on either side towards its outer end. On each side of the passage were intercommunicating rooms for porters and janitors, those to the south giving access to the two turret staircases. For convenience of access within the castle when all the doors and portcullises of the passage were closed, there was also an outside stair, as at Harlech, between the courtyard and the rooms on the first floor. Here at Beaumaris this communicated through the lower part of the westernmost of the five windows,

First-floor entrance through the lower part of the westernmost window (left of picture).

The central window of the North Gatehouse.

which accordingly has a lower sill than the others; the stair's former presence no doubt accounts for the small size of the window openings of the adjoining basement, in contrast to the single large opening on the other side. All five windows were originally mullioned and transomed, as may be seen from the surviving transom in the easternmost window. There is a perceptible

Illustration of the easternmost window of the North Gatehouse (Illustration by John Banbury).

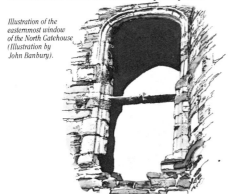

difference between the upper and lower parts of all the windows, but the upper dressings appear to be of one build with the surrounding stonework which in turn supports the bases of the intended windows of the unbuilt second floor; the upper parts of the lower windows are themselves therefore unlikely to be later than the end of the main building period, i.e. c.1330.

As left at that time, the first-floor accommodation towards the courtyard appears to have comprised a single hall, approximately 70 feet by 25 feet (21m by 7.5m). But the position of the two fireplaces suggests that as at Harlech a dividing cross-wall was intended on the line of the eastern side of the passage below, giving a large 'three-windowed' room to the west and a smaller 'two-windowed' room to the east. Visitors can reach the upper levels of the gatehouse by either of two staircases in its western half or by the wall-walk along the western curtain. From different points of vantage many details can be seen, amongst which the following may be noted: (i) the corbels or brackets which supported the timber wall-posts that carried the roof of the hall,

Corbels for timber wall-posts.

and, in its western half, the springers for an unbuilt stone arch which would have supported the intended second floor; (ii) in the south wall, the bases of the embrasures and window seats of the five intended second floor windows; (iii) on

Bases of second floor windows
(Illustration by Delyth Lloyd).

the end walls, faint indications of the outline of the hall's low-pitched roof and (iv) similar indications of the slope of the pent roof which covered as much as was built of the rooms in the two northern towers and over the gate passage;

Two-light window in the east tower of the North Gatehouse.

(v) the large two-light trefoil-headed mullioned and transomed windows in the three top rooms, the smaller and plainer single lights of the rooms below them, and in each room a fireplace, an indication in the case of the two centre rooms above the passage that these were not designed, as the corresponding rooms at Harlech were, to

Top : *Fireplace and window on the upper floor of the eastern tower of the North Gatehouse.*
Above: *Door in the south-west stair turret*
(Illustration by Delyth Lloyd).

serve as chapels; (vi) on the west, one of the small wooden platforms connecting the gatehouse to the curtains at wall-walk level or, if removed, isolating the one from the other; (vii) in the south-west stair turret a door which communicated at first-floor level with the now vanished range of buildings on the west side of the courtyard.

The South Gatehouse

It is clear that in essentials the South Gatehouse was planned to be the close counterpart of the North, to which in the symmetrical layout of the castle it is set axially opposite. But even though the part of it projecting into the courtyard may once have stood slightly higher than now (plate on page 15), it is certain that the building as a whole never achieved anything even approaching the degree of completeness of its far from finished northern replica. Whereas the great outward flanking towers of the North Gatehouse were, as we have seen, carried up at least in part to their full intended height, those of the South Gatehouse never rose beyond the level of the curtain walls to either side of them; thus even towards the front, where the gatehouse is at its highest, we have to envisage the addition of a whole upper storey and battlements to the twin towers. The stair turrets towards the courtyard, now little more than shapeless stumps of masonry, would have risen to a height of something like 70 feet (21m). Small wonder that of the sum of £684 estimated to be needed for repairing and completing the castle in 1343, no less than £320 (£200 of it masons' work) was said to be required for the South Gatehouse (plate on page 15).

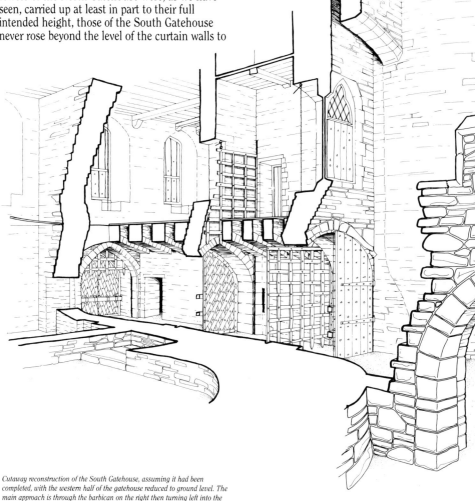

Cutaway reconstruction of the South Gatehouse, assuming it had been completed, with the western half of the gatehouse reduced to ground level. The main approach is through the barbican on the right then turning left into the main gate passage through a succession of obstacles to the interior of the castle on the far left (Illustration by Chris Jones-Jenkins).

The Chapel

The chapel occupies the first floor of the tower on the east side of the inner ward and is now reached by a modern timber staircase leading directly up from the courtyard. Originally, however, the imposing arched doorway at the top of the stairs was designed to be an internal one, reached from and enclosed within the walls of the demolished (or possibly unbuilt) range occupying the northern end of this side of the ward. The position of the chapel as an annexe to that range

Interior of chapel.

suggests that the latter, including the adjacent North-East Tower, was intended to provide the castle's principal residential suite, corresponding to the royal apartments in the inner ward at Conwy.

The chapel proper is entered through twin doorways with trefoiled heads, opening from a lobby communicating at each end with the eastern wall passage as well as with the formerly adjoining rooms against the curtain. It has a semi-octagonal east end and is ceiled with a ribbed stone vault; above the remains of a stone bench, panels of triple blind arcading decorate the lower part of the walls, while the upper part contains five deeply set lancet windows. There are indications of a former western gallery, connected through openings in the north and south walls to small chambers on either side of the chapel, from the northern of which a squint has been cut to command a view of the altar. In the west wall there is an air shaft sloping steeply upward to the wall-walk above. Outside, in the angle between the Chapel Tower and the curtain wall to the south, and visible only from the outer ward, is a small corbelled projection perhaps intended, like a similar feature at Rhuddlan, to house a bell. The chapel is built over a barrel-vaulted basement, while its own vault would have carried the floor of the tower's unfinished top storey, of which only a few feet of the walls were ever built. The cost of completing it was estimated in 1343 at £128, but work was evidently never resumed.

Wall passages and flanking towers

The curtain walls at Beaumaris are throughout pierced at main or first-floor level by long passages similar to those which are such a marked characteristic of Caernarfon. Their purpose was to provide through internal communication between the rooms in the flanking towers and also to give access to the latrines contrived beside them in the thickness of the walls (p.38). The passages are roofed with flat shouldered vaults composed of roughly shaped flag stones carried on running brackets corbelled out from the tops of the side walls; possibly it is these flagstones that are referred to in the 1296 Pipe Roll account as *petras velosas* ('sail stones'), 19,706 tons of them being brought by sea from the quarry* to the castle in the summer of that year at a cost of £164 4s. 4d. or 2d. a ton.

Wall passage in eastern inner curtain wall, running south from the chapel to the South-East Tower.

Cutaway section of the curtain wall of the inner ward between the South-West Tower and the South Gatehouse showing a system of interconnecting latrines at three levels, the uppermost being on the wall-walk (Illustration by Chris Jones-Jenkins).

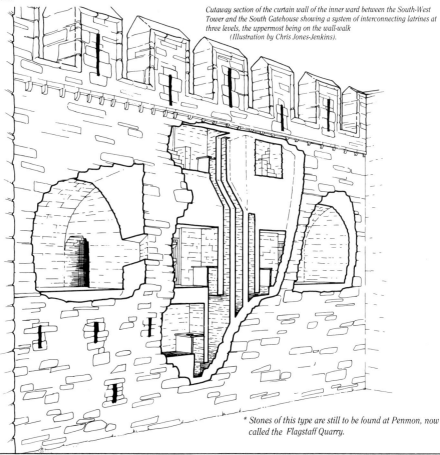

* Stones of this type are still to be found at Penmon, now called the Flagstaff Quarry.

Flat shouldered vault of a guardroom roof near the South-East Tower (Illustration by Delyth Lloyd).

Today these passages can only be reached by circular staircases leading up from the south-west and south-east corners of the inner ward; there are corresponding stairs in the two northern corners and in the middle of the western side, but being partly ruined these latter are now inaccessible. Nor is the circuit of the passages any longer continuous, owing to the floors being destroyed in both the great north and south gatehouses. To reach the eastern passage the visitor should enter from the south-east corner of the courtyard where the left-hand door from the bottom landing leads to the newel staircase; at the next landing turn right again to gain the main

Latrine off wall passage in east curtain wall.

east passage. This can be followed right through to the east tower of the North Gatehouse; doors on the right lead in succession to two latrines, to the chapel and its two side vestibules (from the further of which stairs lead on up to the wall-walk), and finally on the left to a further pair of latrines serving the North-East Tower and the eastern side of the North Gatehouse. Small guardrooms or sleeping chambers in the thickness of the wall are found close beside the South-East and North-East Towers, the vaulted roof in the former case being gathered over from no fewer than six corbel courses on either side; in one case as many as seven courses of corbelling are used.

Guardroom near South-East Tower.

The narrowing of the passage between the Chapel and the North-East Tower is where it passes behind the fireplaces of the adjacent Great Hall and Chamber. The passage in the western wall is approached from the south-west corner of the courtyard and there are similar openings to latrines and wall chambers along its whole half-circuit from gatehouse to gatehouse.

In addition to the two gatehouses six round or half-round towers flank the curtains of the inner ward; the South-East, Chapel and North-East

Towers to the right and the South-West, Middle and North-West Towers to the left as the visitor enters the castle. The Chapel having been described already (p.33), attention is here drawn to the principal features of the remaining towers.

The basement and first-floor of the South-West Tower.

Apart from the Chapel Tower with its stone floor and vault, all the others are without roofs and floors of any kind. All were designed to be three storeys high, but the top storey was only partly built in the case of the three eastern towers and to an even lesser extent in the case of those on the west. The four corner towers are all octagonal internally above the ground stage, which is circular; the Chapel and Middle towers are semi-octagonal internally at all levels. In the corner

The basement of the Middle Tower.

towers the circular basements are restricted for light and air to a single vent shaft sloping steeply up through the thickness of the walls to a narrow slit and can only have been intended as prisons.

The first-floor, basement and stone diaphragm arch of the South-East Tower.

Stone diaphragm arches (complete in the South-East and remaining partially in the South-West and North-East towers) may indicate an exceptionally strong and heavy floor above each basement. In the North-East Tower there is also a complete diaphragm arch over the main room. In each tower the principal chamber was on the first or middle floor and was lit by a two-light mullioned window similar to the top-floor windows at Conwy, and warmed from a handsome hooded fireplace; in every case subordinate rooms and latrines were at hand, reached throughout this level by way of the connecting passages. Sufficient of the second-floor rooms was built on the South-East and Chapel towers to show that

Hooded fireplace at first-floor level in the South-East Tower.

they would have closely resembled those below them. In the Chapel Tower the ground stage has a stone barrel-vaulted roof; the Middle Tower on the opposite side of the courtyard has a well-preserved diaphragm arch at ground level, while its main floor has a fireplace and blocked two-light window like those in the corner towers.

Wall-walks and latrines

The staircases at the south-east and south-west corners of the courtyard may be used to reach the wall-top level of the curtains which with little variation is maintained round the perimeters of the unfinished corner towers and those of the South Gatehouse. The paving of the wall walks with beach pebbles dates from the time of the Office of Works renovations in the 1920s and 30s,

prior to which the wall tops supported a rich growth of trees and verdure: so luxuriant, indeed, that the vaulted roof of the Chapel Tower was known to the local boys as the 'orchard' on account of its well-grown crab tree.* The remains of the battlements are fragmentary; only six out of an original thirty-six merlons still retain their loops complete, but enough is left to show that, as at the other North Wales castles, these were set at alternating levels of declination so as to give command over differing fields of fire.

* Information given in 1978 by Mr. James Parry of Beaumaris (b.1904).

Right: *Battlements with their arrowloops on the curtain wall between the South-East Tower and the South Gatehouse.*
Below: *Staircase in the south-west corner of the North Gatehouse.*

The most conspicuous feature of the Beaumaris wall-walks is the presence of the latrines which are placed in pairs, two pairs to each of the long sides and one to each of the four short northern and southern sides, making sixteen latrines in all at this level in addition to the sixteen accessible from the wall passages below. Their ingenious construction repays examination. Within its 15

individual cubicles; these are approached down an angled flight of six or more steps, at the bottom of which privacy was afforded by a door neatly rebated against the wall; in many cases the stumps of the door's iron hinges, carefully run in lead, can still be seen; beyond the door is the

Wall-walk latrines in the southern half of the west inner curtain wall (Illustration by Delyth Lloyd).

feet 6 inches (4.65m) thickness each section of wall houses a large rectangular pit extending from below ground level to the wall walk. Above the pits there are set back to back at each level a pair of latrine seats, separated one from the other by a continuous rectangular ventilating shaft rising from the centre of the pit to the outside air. The design is unique to Beaumaris and is almost certainly related to the castle's being placed at sea channels now long blocked beneath the outer ward, much as channels under the outer ward run from the latrine pits to discharge into the dry moat at Rhuddlan. The latrines open position on the wall walk allows us to see the planning of the

Plan of wall-walk latrines

Position of door   Position of door

BATTLEMENTS

Steps   Steps

Seat   Seat
Ventilating shaft

← WALL WALK →

0   30 feet

The iron stump of the original hinge within a rebate for a latrine cubicle door.

latrine proper, the groove for its wooden seat set in the walls of a little recess, with the air shaft behind separating it from its immediately adjoining neighbour. The latrines and their flushing system were already a cause of concern at the time of John de Metfield's survey of 1306: amongst others of the castle's serious shortcomings (*grevuse defautes*) it was reported that 'the 'little houses' (*les petites Mesones*) in the body of the castle needed to be roofed over (in other words then as now they were open to the sky), their drains (*gutteres*) required repairing and mending, and the said houses needed to be cleansed of refuse (*fer' nettor de ordure*), the ducts (*les ussues*) of the latrines being full of water and filth' (PRO, E 101 486/20).

Exterior of inner ward and interior of outer ward

It is in the nature of a concentrically planned castle such as Beaumaris that, when the visitor is in the outer ward, he sees on the one hand the outside of the great walls and towers of the inner ward and on the other the inside of the lower walls and towers of the outer. In this section it is proposed to point out first some of the features worth noting when perambulating the inner wall before turning attention to the outer, starting from the South-West Tower and proceeding northwards. Notice that in all three western towers the large two-light windows are blocked with stone, only the South-East Tower window being both unblocked and retaining its centre

Right: *Blocked two-light window in the North-West Tower.*
Below: *View of the western side of the outer ward looking north towards the Middle Tower from the South-West Tower.*

mullion; the probability is that the corresponding windows in the North-East Tower and the four gate towers, all of which have lost their mullions, have also lost former blockings. Here we may note too that in the whole circuit of the outer walls and towers a great many of the arrow slits at ground level, no fewer than 79 out of a total of 164, are also wholly or partially blocked, and it is likely that at some time in the history of the castle this blocking of the outer ring loops was universal. Such a security measure must date either from the Glyndŵr troubles of c.1405 or from the Civil War in the seventeenth century, but there is now no evidence to suggest which. Looking again at the inner ring, we may be struck by the notable regularity of the moulded stone

Detail of moulded stone corbel table on outer face of inner curtain wall.

corbel tables at wall-top level all round the main curtains, giving a decorative finish that in some measure compensates for the evident incompleteness of the towers. Good examples of evidence for the constructional use of inclined scaffold paths can be seen in the sloping lines of

Sloping line of putlog holes on eastern tower of North Gatehouse.

putlog holes on the eastern North Gatehouse tower, the North-East Tower and the curtains to either side of it. Note the bellcote in the south angle of the Chapel Tower; note also the well-preserved carving of one of two gargoyle head

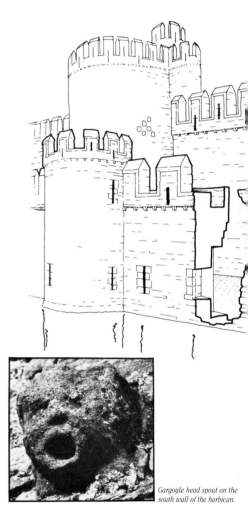

Gargoyle head spout on the south wall of the barbican.

spouts on the south wall of the barbican. The barbican itself was built as a hindrance to any possibility of any enemy rushing the main South Gatehouse at a time when not only the gatehouse itself was unfinished but the south outer curtain and Gate Next the Sea may also very likely still have stood short of their full intended height.

Reconstruction and cutaway view of the south-west corner of the castle showing both the outer and inner lines of defence (Illustration by Chris Jones-Jenkins).

Simple in its symmetrical eight-sided layout, the outer curtain with its numerous flanking towers and two twin-towered gateways is none the less a complex and remarkable piece of construction, remarkable in particular for the completeness of its survival in contrast to the fragmentary state of the corresponding works at Aberystwyth, Harlech and Rhuddlan, so that in Wales Beaumaris is the concentric castle *par excellence*. Space precludes our describing it in detail. Suffice to point out that as an outer

obstacle to attack it had an offensive purpose also, in that its arrow loops provided firing points in every direction at three levels from the turrets and two from the linking curtains. The crenellation, i.e. the battlementing with the top level of loops, has almost wholly perished, but it is calculated that when complete this outer circuit of fortification was equipped with not far short of 300 positions from any group of which the defending garrison could harass attackers at whatever point they might concentrate their assault. The survey of 1343 (p.47) reported 30 perches of the castle walls as being 'partly ruinous.' If the reference was to the outer curtain, it may be that the section strengthened by the addition of internal arches to the west of the Gate Next the Sea was included and that the arches are a remedial measure carried out at that time. It is noticeable that the length of wall eastwards from the Gate Next the Sea to the south-east corner shows a slight inward lean, but these two lengths together are still a good deal short of 30 perches. The whole circuit of the outer wall walk is accessible to visitors and all turrets can be entered at ground level.

Exterior of outer ward

It may be recalled that the progress report of February 1296 (Appendix I, p.46) indicated that only ten of the outer turrets were included in the initial construction works begun in the previous year. From outside the castle the observant visitor will be able to detect the points at which this earliest construction was subsequently linked with later work, and heightened throughout to produce the outer curtain as we see it today. The ten towers mentioned in the record of 1296 commence with the tower numbered 1 on the plan at the end of the guide and continue anti-clockwise to the tower numbered 10 at the north-east corner. The first work appears only to have reached a height of about 8 feet (2.4m) above moat water level, where for much of the intervening distance there is a well-marked horizontal break or change-line in the masonry.

Internal arches in outer curtain wall to west of the 'Gate next the Sea'.

Horizontal break or change-line in the masonry of the outer curtain wall to west of 'Gate next the Sea'.

Everywhere below this line the arrow loops are distinctive in having dressed stone jambs or sides but no dressed stone lintel. Above it the loops on all the towers, and throughout the section subsequently built to complete the circuit on the north and west (between Tower 10 and Tower 1), have dressed stone lintels as well as dressed jambs and bases. All this later work must belong to the period after 1306 and before 1330, but it cannot be dated more closely. The outer curtain can be viewed from across the moat on the north, the west and south-west sides, and from the recreation ground outside the castle on the east.

An arrowloop without a dressed stone lintel, below the horizontal break in the masonry.

An arrowloop with a dressed stone lintel, jambs and base, above the horizontal break in the masonry.

Castle dock and Gunners Walk

The 1296 record shows that the dock was planned from the beginning to make the castle accessible to sea-going shipping, the door in its end wall enabling a boat to unload straight into the castle. The 12 foot (3.6m) wide 'Gunners Walk' was built to revet the eastern side of the dock and to afford a shooting deck with arrow loops and battlements on either side. A raised machicolated platform at its southern end may well have been the position of a trebuchet or stone-throwing catapult. The tower projecting from Gunners Walk into the dock contains the remains of a water mill and the sluice controlling the flow of tidal water to and from the moat. The name 'Gunners Walk' appears to date only from the mid nineteenth century.

Platform at the southern end of Gunners Walk.

Gunners Walk with the castle dock on the right (Illustration by Delyth Lloyd).

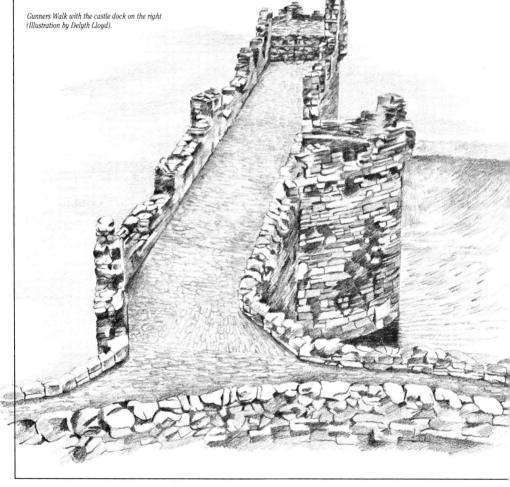

Purpose of residential accommodation

No thinking visitor will leave Beaumaris castle without pausing to wonder for whom so much accommodation was planned and considered necessary: the great hall and chamber indicated by the fireplaces in the north-east part of the courtyard, not one but two similar halls and chambers (though only one of them was ever built) in the North Gatehouse, and two corresponding halls and chambers (neither of them built) in the South Gatehouse, five self-contained suites in all. Had they been completed the twin towers of the two gatehouses, the four corner towers, the Middle Tower and the top of the Chapel Tower would have added another nineteen good rooms, all warmed and well lit and each with its private latrine along the passage. What was it all for?

A short answer would be to say that something of this order must have been what was envisaged in 1295 as providing the minimum required to accommodate the king and queen and their households, if the king should marry again and if the court should wish to make a stay in Anglesey, and perhaps we should not attempt to look further than this. But we may remind ourselves that Edward of Caernarfon was now entering his twelfth year, and a time might not lie far ahead when it would be additionally convenient to have fitting apartments appropriated to a prince and princess and their attendant households as well as to a king and future queen. There was also the constable of the castle, whether resident with his family or represented by a deputy. And where, if not in Beaumaris Castle, was the office of the sheriff of Anglesey? Conwy, a walled town from the first, had its 'King's Hall', its 'Prince's Hall', its justiciar's lodging, its tower 'assigned for the lodging of the chamberlain', all of them outside the castle but within the protection of the town walls. In 1295 Beaumaris would have no town walls for a century and more to come: may it be reasonable to suggest that some of the chambers, perhaps some of the suites, in the castle were planned with corresponding needs and claims in mind? As to lesser officials, the little fireplaced rooms in the corner turrets of the outer ward and over the Gate Next the Sea must have been well suited for the comfort and convenience of the porters and the janitors.

Further Reading

Principal sources and books for further reading

J.G. Edwards, 'Edward I's Castle-building in Wales', *Proceedings of the British Academy*, 33 (1946), 15-81.

A.J. Taylor, *The King's Works in Wales, 1277-1330* (London, HMSO, 1974).

E.A. Lewis, *The Medieval Boroughs of Snowdonia* (London, 1912).

J.E. Lloyd, *Owen Glendower* (Oxford, 1931).

H. Rees Davies, *The Conway and the Menai Ferries* (Cardiff, 1942).

Inventory of Ancient Monuments in Anglesey (RCAHM Wales, 1937), 1-13 and cxlviii-ix.

C.M. Evans, 'The Medieval Borough of Beaumaris, 1200-1600' (unpublished MA thesis in library of University College of North Wales, Bangor).

E. Neaverson, 'Medieval Castles in North Wales, a study of sites, water supply and building stones' (Liverpool, 1947, 50-51.

Appendix 1

Letter of 27 February, 1296 from James of St George and Walter of Winchester at Conwy to the Treasurer and Barons of the Exchequer at Westminister.

**Aberconewey,
27 February 1296**

To their very dear lordships the Treasurer and Barons of the Exchequer of our lord the King, James of St. George and Walter of Winchester send greeting and due reverence.

Sirs,

As our lord the king has commanded us, by letters of the exchequer, to let you have a clear picture of all aspects of the state of the works at Beaumaris, so that you may be able to lay down the level of work (ordiner lestat de loevre) *for this coming season as may seem best to you, we write to inform you that the work we are doing is very costly and we need a great deal of money.*

You should know:

(i) That we have kept on masons, stone cutters, quarrymen and minor workmen all through the winter, and are still employing them, for making mortar and breaking up stone for lime; we have had carts bringing this stone to the site and bringing timber for erecting the buildings in which we are all now living inside the castle (a edifier en chastel la ou nous sumes touz demorrantz ore); *we also have 1,000 carpenters, smiths, plasterers and navvies, quite apart from a mounted garrison of 10 men accounting for 70s. a week, 20 cross-bowmen who add another 47s. 10d. and 100 infantry who take a further £6 2s. 6d.*

(ii) That when this letter was written, we were short of £500, for both workmen and garrison. The men's pay has been and still is very much in arrear, and we are having the greatest difficulty in keeping them because they simply have nothing to live on.

(iii) That if our lord the king wants the work to be finished as quickly as it should be on the scale on which it has been commenced (que loevre se perfate vistement ausi come mestie serreit e sicome ele est comencee), *we could not make do with less than £250 a week throughout the season; with it, this season could see the work well advanced. If, however, you feel we cannot have so much money, let us know, and we will put the workmen at your disposal according to whatever you think will be the best profit of our lord the king.*

As for the progress of the work, we have sent a previous report to the king. We can tell you that some of it already stands about 28 feet high and even where it is lowest it is 20 feet. We have begun 10 of the outer and four of the inner towers, i.e. the two for each of the two gatehouse passages (si sont comence x tours dehors e quatre dedens, a chescune porte deus pur les ales'). *Four gates have been hung and are shut and locked every night, and each gateway is to have three portcullises. You should also know that at high tide a 40-ton vessel will be able to come fully laden right up to the castle gateway; so much have we been able to do in spite of all the Welshmen* (maugre touz les Galeys tant avons nous fait).

In case you should wonder where so much money could go in a week, we would have you know that we have needed — and shall continue to need — 400 masons, both cutters and layers, together with 2,000 minor workmen, 100 carts (charettes), *60 waggons* (carres) *and 30 boats bringing stone and sea-coal; 200 quarrymen; 30 smiths; and carpenters for putting in the joists and floor-boards and other necessary jobs. All this takes no account of the garrison mentioned above, nor of purchases of materials, of which there will have to be a great quantity.*

As to how things are in the land of Wales, we still cannot be any too sure (de lestat de la terre de Gales nous nensavons uncore si bien nony). *But, as you well know, Welshmen are Welshmen, and you need to understand them properly; if, which God forbid, there is a war with France and Scotland, we shall need to watch them all the more closely* (font a duter de tant le plus).

You may be assured, dear sirs, that we shall make it our business to give satisfaction in everything.

May God protect you dearest lordships.

P.S. And, Sirs, for God's sake be quick with the money for the works, as much as ever our lord the king wills; otherwise everything done up till now will have been of no avail (tout come ilyad fait uncore poy vaut si plus nysoit fait).

**(Public Record Office, E 101/5/18, no.11;
original in Norman French).**

Appendix 2

William de Emeldon's Survey, 1343

In June 1343 William de Emeldon was appointed to investigate the state of the king's principal castles in Wales, five castles in the north (Conwy, Beaumaris, Caernarfon, Criccieth and Harlech) and nine in the south and west (Aberystwyth, Emlyn, Cardigan, Haverfordwest, Carmarthen, Dryslwyn, Dinefwr, Builth and Montgomery). The reports of the inquiry are preserved in the Public Record Office (E 163/4/42), that on the state of the fabric of Beaumaris being as follows:

By inquisition held there in the presence of the said William on 3rd August 1343, into the defects of the said castle of Beaumaris, it is found:

1   *That a certain chamber over the gate next the sea is dilapidated and ruinous and can be repaired and mended for £7, viz. for stonework £2, for timber and carpentry £3, and for leadwork and other necessaries £2.*

2   *That the roofs and floors of two chambers in the double tower* ('le Gemell Tour') *are badly dilapidated and ruinous through rotted timbers and lack of roofing, and can be repaired and mended for £35, viz. £25 for masonry and stonework, £8 for woodwork, and £2 for leadwork and other necessaries.*

3   *That the roof of the hall and of the chamber of the same hall can be repaired and mended in lead for 13s. 4d.*

4   *That a tower called 'Rustycoker' is ruinous for want of a roof and can be roofed and mended for an estimated £8, viz. £4 for stonework and £4 for leadwork and other necessaries.*

5   *That a tower called 'le Capeltoure' which is begun and not finished can be completed for £128, all works included.*

6   *That a tower called 'Pilardesbathe' is dilapidated and ruinous owing to the rotting of its timber and roof, and can be roofed with slates (cum tegulis) and mended where otherwise necessary for £10, viz. £5 for stonework, £3 for carpentry and £2 for slates and other works.*

7   *That a tower called 'le Gyntour' is in very great need of repair, and can be repaired and mended for £10, viz. £5 for stonework, £3 for timber and carpentry, and £2 for leadwork and other necessaries.*

8   *That Three* (sic) *towers called 'Gemelles Toures' (lit. 'twin' or 'double' towers) above the inner gatehouse* (super portam interiorem) *of the said castle can be roofed and mended for £15, viz. £9 for carpentry and woodwork and £6 for lead for the roofs.*

9   *That a tower called 'le Mideltoure' can be roofed and repaired for £5, viz. £3 for timber and carpentry and £2 for roofing in lead.*

10   *That a tower which stands at the corner of the castle towards the meadow* (in angulo castri versus pratum) *can be repaired and mended for £10, viz. £5 for stonework, £3 for timber and carpentry, and £2 for lead for the roof.*

11   *That 30 perches* (rode) *of the walls of the said castle which are partly ruinous can be repaired for £30.*

12   *That is is estimated that two towers and two chambers on the inner gatehouse of the said castle, which begun and not finished cannot be completed for less than £200 for stone and stonework, £80 for timber and carpentry, and £40 for leadwork and other necessaries.*

13   *That the kitchen, which is dilapidated and ruinous for lack of repair and want of a roof, cannot be repaired and mended for less than 10 marks (£6 13s. 4d.) for all works.*

14   *To complete two towers above the hall to height of (blank in MS.) including the height of the existing towers as they now stand* (cum turribus assistentibus), *£100 for stone and stonework.*

Sum of the defects of the wall, houses, towers and other buildings of the said castle, £684 6s. 8d.

Some of the foregoing paragraphs are more easily identifiable than others. Paragraph 1 is self-explanitory, while paragraph 11 also seems more likely to refer to the outer than to the inner curtain wall. Paragraphs 4 and 6, placed as they are in sequence on either side of the Chapel Tower, are likely to relate to the towers on either side of it, i.e. the North-East and South-East Towers, but which of these was called 'Rustycoker' and which 'Pilardesbathe' is impossible to say, nor can the names themselves be satisfactorily explained. The placing of paragraph 7 before and of paragraph 10 immediately after the Middle Tower paragraph similarly suggests that the 'tower at the corner towards the meadow' must be the North-West Tower, and by elimination 'le Gyntour' would thus seem to be the South-West Tower; the name may be Welsh 'gwyn' tower, i.e. white tower. It is to be noted that of all these six towers only one, the Chapel Tower, is recommended for completion, at an estimated cost of £28, it evidently being considered that the others need only be made good as they stand, at costs estimated at from £5 to £10 each.

Besides the estimate for the Chapel Tower there are three other estimates for work involving resumed construction in stone. The largest of these is in paragraph 12, and this with its very high figure of £320 must surely represent the cost of completing the building of the South Gatehouse. Paragraph 14, at £100 for stonework only, must correspondingly relate to the North Gatehouse, and more particularly to the carrying of its two half-built staircase towers up to their full planned height. Paragraph 2 seems also likely to refer to the North Gatehouse, more particularly to finishing off (and closing off at their backs) the twin towers flanking the outer end of the gate passage. The hall and chamber named in paragraph 3 could be either the hall and chamber on the first floor of the rearward part of the North Gatehouse, or the hall and chamber whose fireplaces remain in the curtain wall between the North-East Tower and the Chapel Tower; but it is not possible to say which of the two is intended. Paragraph 8 seems most likely, by the process of elimination, to refer to the built part of the South Gatehouse, i.e. to re-roofing at existing level the rooms in its flanking towers with the connecting rooms over the gate passage between them. The kitchen named in paragraph 13 is evidently a separate building; it probably stood against the northern part of the west curtain wall.

It seems fairly certain that none of the major items involving the resumption of structural work on buildings previously left unfinished was put in hand. The arched thickening of the outer curtain between the south-west corner and the 'Gate Next the Sea' may possibly have resulted from the recommendation made in paragraph 11. No evidence has survived to show whether any or all of the less expensive repairs to roofs, etc., were effected as a result of the survey or not.